★ **PIPPA P....** ★

MY
JOURNAL
About Life

By ....
(name)

With help from
Pippa Park & Erin Yun

FABLED FILMS PRESS
NEW YORK CITY

Published by Fabled Films LLC, New York

ISBN: 978-1-944020-68-2

First Edition: September 2021

1 3 5 7 9 10 8 6 4 2

Author: Erin Yun
Project Managed by Nicole Wheeler
Editorial Support: Dienesa Le, Micah White
Design Support: Chris Chew, Samantha Sicignano
Cover Designed by Jaime Mendola-Hobbie
Illustrations by Bev Johnson, Sharon Shields Lee
Interior Book Design by Lauren Woodrow
Printed by Everbest in China

FABLED FILMS PRESS
NEW YORK CITY

fabledfilms.com

For information on bulk purchases for promotional use, please
contact Consortium Book Sales & Distribution sales department at
ingrampublishersvcs@ingramcontent.com or 1-866-400-5351.

CELEBRATE THE REAL YOU

with this *Pippa Park* fill-in journal.
Packed full of awesome quizzes, listicles,
and writing prompts, this is a place for
you to explore your thoughts about you,
your family, friends, school, and what you
like and dislike! This is a record of what
makes your life unique. Hope you have fun
writing and sharing your discoveries.

ABOUT PIPPA

Name: Pippa Park

Nickname: Pips and Gangaji

Age: 12

Birthday: April 14th

Favorite Color: red

Favorite Food: kimchi-jjigae and walnut cakes

Favorite Animal: lion

Hobbies: basketball, TV, and cooking

3 Adjectives to Describe Me: sporty, ambitious, and funny

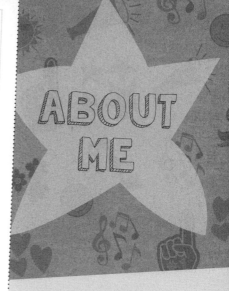

ABOUT ME

Attach or draw a picture of yourself here!

Name: ....

Nickname: ....

Age: ....

Birthday: ....

Favorite Color: ....

Favorite Food: ....

Favorite Animal: ....

Hobbies: ....

3 Adjectives to Describe Me: ....

....

THIS OR THAT?

I am...

Circle the item in each pair that you feel best describes you.

Tall	‹····· or ·····›	Short
Neat	‹····· or ·····›	Messy
Shy	‹····· or ·····›	Outgoing
Graceful	‹····· or ·····›	Clumsy
Hyper	‹····· or ·····›	Laid-Back
Adventurous	‹····· or ·····›	Cautious
Silly	‹····· or ·····›	Serious
Logical	‹····· or ·····›	Emotional
Imaginative	‹····· or ·····›	Realistic

THE 5-WORD CHALLENGE

Think of just 5 words to describe yourself. Ask family and friends to do the same and compare.

5 WORDS to
Describe Yourself!

1. _____
2. _____
3. _____
4. _____
5. _____

Ask Your Family
to Choose **5 WORDS**
to Describe You!

1. _____
2. _____
3. _____
4. _____
5. _____

Ask Your Friends
to Choose **5 WORDS**
to Describe You!

1. _____
2. _____
3. _____
4. _____
5. _____

THE REAL ME

What do you wish people knew about the real you?

ME, MYSELF, AND I

What do you like most about yourself?

Draw or paste a picture here!

WHICH *PIPPA PARK* CHARACTER ARE YOU?

Pippa and her friends are full of personality—and so are you!
Take the quiz to find out which character you are in *Pippa Park
Raises Her Game.*

 You are at the park playing basketball and hear
live music coming from the woods. You

   a. search for the musician—they can't be too far!

   b. keep playing, this time with some nice background music.

   c. head home to give the musician space to express himself
   or herself.

 Your backpack is

   a. messy! You can get to your textbooks,
   but it might take some work.

   b. a snack attack! Always plenty for you and your friends.

   c. more than just a backpack! It's a fashion statement.

 In class, you play the role of

   a. daydreamer.   **b.** class clown.   **c.** royalty.

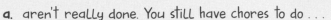

 4 You are all done with your homework! You
   a. aren't really done. You still have chores to do . . .
   b. turn on your favorite TV show and grab the popcorn.
   c. video chat the squad to make plans for the weekend.

 5 Your friend is having a hard time. You
   a. check in to see how they are but give them space.
   b. surprise them with a day of *all* their favorite things.
   c. talk it out over mani-pedis.

 6 Your friends would describe you as
   a. spunky.   b. caring.   c. talented.

 7 But your friends would hesitate to call you
   a. organized.   b. over-the-top.   c. patient.

 8 Your family says you can have a holiday party! You
   a. don't know who to invite until it's too late. Oh well, maybe next time?
   b. call your BFF. It's a party whenever you are together.
   c. jump on party planning. It'll be the talk of the school!

Count how many A's, B's, and C's you chose on the quiz to reveal which *Pippa Park* character you are on the next page!

A	B	C

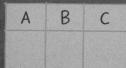

RESULTS! YOU ARE . . .

MOSTLY A'S ☐

← Put a check next to the character you are most like!

PIPPA

You are a **CURIOUS DREAMER**. Your **BRAVERY** and **AMBITION** leave you in messes sometimes, but your **SPUNK** and **POSITIVE ATTITUDE** can get you through **ANYTHING**!

MOSTLY B'S ☐

BUDDY

You are **FUN** and **EASYGOING**. Always there with a snack or helping hand—your **GENEROSITY** does not go unnoticed, and with your **LOYALTY**? Anyone would be lucky to call you a **FRIEND**.

MOSTLY C'S ☐

BIANCA

You are **DEDICATED** and **DRIVEN**, which makes you an **INSPIRING** friend! You are a **NATURAL-BORN LEADER**—both on and off the court—and you can make even a school uniform look **TRENDY**.

Color in the bar to show how much you agree with your quiz results on a scale of 1-10.

| 1 | 2 | 3 | 4 | 5 | 6 | 7 | 8 | 9 | 10 |

Absolutely not!   Makes sense.   Exactly right!

What did the quiz get **RIGHT**?

What did the quiz get **WRONG**?

SHARE THE QUIZ!

Which *Pippa Park* character would your family and friends be? Ask them to take the quiz, and then fill in their results below!

NAME	IS MOST LIKE . . .

THINK HAPPY THOUGHTS

What makes you happy? Fill in the clouds with words or drawings of everything that makes you smile, laugh, and enjoy the day.

BLOW OUT THE CANDLES

What traditions are part of your birthday celebration every year?

YOU SHOULDN'T HAVE!

Imagine you open a present to find exactly what you've always wanted inside. Draw or write about it below.

MY ABSOLUTELY PERFECT DREAM DAY

What would your perfect day look like? Draw your dream day from morning until night!

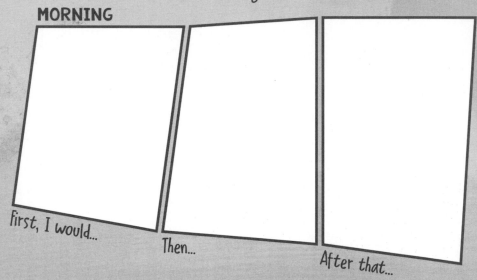

MORNING

First, I would...

Then...

After that...

AFTERNOON

First, I would...

Then...

After that...

EVENING

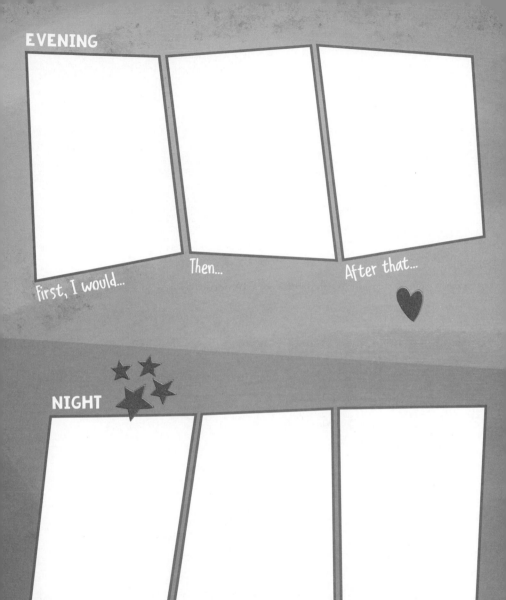

First, I would...

Then...

After that...

NIGHT

First, I would...

Then...

After that...

19

FIND YOUR PERSONAL STYLE!

Whether you care about fashion or not, personal style is a great way to express yourself. Take the quiz to find out what style fits your personality.

 Your go-to piece of clothing is a

a. comfy sweatshirt.

b. cute, patterned dress.

c. perfect pair of jeans.

 You are best described as

a. easygoing.   b. extra.   c. graceful.

 Pick one!

a.   b.   c.

 How often do you go shopping?

a. Rarely or never

b. As much as I can

c. When I need something

5 Your ideal Friday night is
   a. chilling at home.
   b. trying something new.
   c. hanging out with friends.

 6 Time to get into PJs. You put on
   a. what you were already wearing.
   b. printed pants and a cute tank.
   c. your go-to matching set.

 7 You'd rather be
   a. sleeping.   b. shopping.   c. reading.

 8 Most of your T-shirts are
   a. oversized.   b. brightly colored.   c. striped.

 9 Your closet is
   a. always open for easy access.
   b. stuffed full and not very neat.
   c. pretty organized.

Count how many A's, B's, and C's you chose on the quiz to reveal your personal style on the next page!

A	B	C

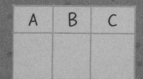

RESULTS! YOUR STYLE IS . . .

MOSTLY A'S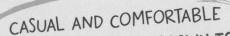

Put a check next to your winning personal style!

CASUAL AND COMFORTABLE

You are **SUPER CHILL** and **DOWN TO EARTH**—and so is your style! Your soft sweatshirts and worn-in sneakers reflect your ability to make **ANYONE** feel just as **COMFORTABLE** when they are with you.

MOSTLY B'S

BOLD AND COLORFUL

You are **CREATIVE** and **IMAGINATIVE**, and it shows in your style! With outfits as **FUN** as your personality, you **LIVEN UP** any room and encourage others to be just as **BOLD**.

MOSTLY C'S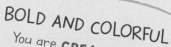

SIMPLE AND CLASSIC

You are **SINCERE** and **RELIABLE**. You know **EXACTLY** what works for you, and your style is **TIMELESS**. You have a signature look that expresses your inner **CONFIDENCE**. It's so you!

QUIZ REFLECTION

Color in the bar to show how much you agree with your
quiz results on a scale of 1-10.

| 1 | 2 | 3 | 4 | 5 | 6 | 7 | 8 | 9 | 10 |

Absolutely not!   Makes sense.   Exactly right!

What did the quiz get **RIGHT**?

What did the quiz get **WRONG**?

SHARE THE QUIZ!

Which personal style fits your family and friends? Ask them to
take the quiz, and then fill in their results below.

NAME	PERSONAL STYLE IS . . .

MY DREAM OUTFIT

If you could wear **ANYTHING** in the whole world right now, what would it be? Draw your dream outfit below!

Don't forget accessories!

Think about colors, patterns, and materials.

WOULD YOU RATHER?

Signature Style

Circle the item in each pair that most reflects your personal style.

Heels	‹····· or ·····›	Sneakers
Pants	‹····· or ·····›	Skirts
Fancy	‹····· or ·····›	Casual
Stripes	‹····· or ·····›	Polka Dots
Jeans	‹····· or ·····›	Leggings
Curly Hair	‹····· or ·····›	Straight Hair
Swimsuit	‹····· or ·····›	Winter Coat
Hair Up	‹····· or ·····›	Hair Down
Neutrals	‹····· or ·····›	Brights

★ ONE AMAZING MOMENT

What is the best thing that has ever happened to you (so far)?

TRIP OF A LIFETIME!

Imagine you are planning a trip. Everything you say goes.
What does your dream trip look like?

DESERT ISLAND

Imagine you are stuck on a desert island. Choose 5 things to eat, watch, and read over and over (and over) again!

I'd eat . . .

1. _____
2. _____
3. _____
4. _____
5. _____

I'd watch . . .

1. _____
2. _____
3. _____
4. _____
5. _____

I'd read . . .

1. _____
2. _____
3. _____
4. _____
5. _____

MY FAVORITE FAMILY TRIP

Write about that one family trip you could never forget and what made it so special.

THANKS a MiLLiON

Think about what you are grateful for—big and small. Fill in the bubbles below with everything that makes your day #BLESSED.

31

ABOUT PIPPA'S FAMILY

Name: Mina Kim

They are my: sister and guardian

Age: 35

Birthday: August 24th

Favorite Color: navy blue

Favorite Food: tteokbokki

Favorite Animal: raven

Hobbies: reading, working, and podcasts

3 Adjectives to Describe Them: responsible, organized, and stubborn

ABOUT PIPPA'S FAMILY

Name: Jung-Hwa Kim

They are my: brother-in-law and guardian

Age: 34

Birthday: July 29th

Favorite Color: yellow and orange

Favorite Food: kimchi-fried rice and ice cream

Favorite Animal: dog

Hobbies: cooking and board games

3 Adjectives to Describe Them: caring, cheerful, and generous

ABOUT MY FAMILY

Attach or draw pictures of your family!

Name:

They are my:

Age:

Birthday:

Favorite Color:

Favorite Food:

Favorite Animal:

Hobbies:

3 Adjectives to Describe Them:

ABOUT MY FAMILY

Name: _____

They are my: _____

Age: _____

Birthday: _____

Favorite Color: _____

Favorite Food: _____

Favorite Animal: _____

Hobbies: _____

3 Adjectives to Describe Them: _____

_____

ABOUT MY FAMILY

Attach or draw pictures of your family!

Name:

They are my:

Age:

Birthday:

Favorite Color:

Favorite Food:

Favorite Animal:

Hobbies:

3 Adjectives to Describe Them:

ABOUT MY FAMILY

Name: _____

They are my: _____

Age: _____

Birthday: _____

Favorite Color: _____

Favorite Food: _____

Favorite Animal: _____

Hobbies: _____

3 Adjectives to Describe Them: _____

_____

INSPIRED BY

Who do you want to be more like in your family? Celebrate the ways you are the same and different below.

I AM INSPIRED BY _____

Ways You're the SAME

- _____
- _____
- _____
- _____
- _____

Ways You're DIFFERENT

- _____
- _____
- _____
- _____
- _____

I hope to be more like my sister, Mina, who is strong, independent, and caring.

Ways You Hope to Be MORE LIKE THEM

- _____
- _____
- _____
- _____
- _____

◈ SECRET ◈ CELEB ◈

You find out you are secretly related to a celebrity.
Who do you want it to be and why?

MY EXTRAORDINARY FAMILY

What makes your family special? Fill in the flowers with words or drawings of everything that makes your family one of a kind.

Think about inside jokes, holiday traditions, or ways your family makes you proud.

41

FUN WITH THE FAM

Having fun together looks different for every family. What do you and your fam like to do? Maybe it's a game, book, show, or place you enjoy together.

Go on road trips

Clean the garage

★ Go on road trips

HOW TO PLAY

1. Fill in the 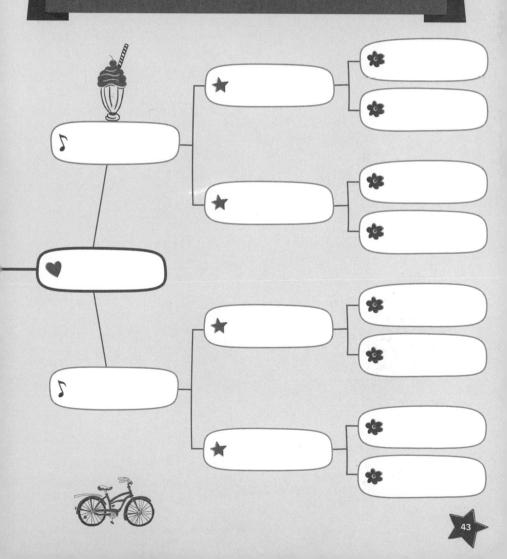 with your favorite things to do as a family! We filled in the first two to get you started.

2. Compare each pair of and select a winner. The winner moves on to the ★ level.

3. Continue on through the ♪ until you have a final ♡ pair. Then select the first-place winner to determine your ultimate family fun-time activity!

43

THAT HOLIDAY FEELING

How do you celebrate your favorite holiday,
and why is it your favorite?

ONLY MY FAMILY

What makes your family unique?

FAMILY FUNNIES

We all have funny stories that get told over and over again.
Capture your favorite family stories by drawing them below!

TITLE: _____

TITLE: _____

TITLE:

TITLE:

CAN'T THINK
OF ONE?
MAKE IT UP!

KIMCHI-JJIGAE

A CLASSIC KOREAN STEW FROM ERIN YUN, AUTHOR OF *PIPPA PARK RAISES HER GAME*

ABOUT MY DISH

Kimchi-jjigae is a warm, cozy stew starring kimchi, a spicy, fermented cabbage. As a kid, I remember digging though my bowl of stew to find the tender bits of pork belly. But it's easy to substitute the pork belly for any protein in your refrigerator! Once the ingredients are prepared and chopped, this dish comes together easily. The biggest challenge? Try not to devour the whole pot in one sitting!

Makes 4 generous servings
Prep time: 15 minutes / Cook time: 40 to 45 minutes

INGREDIENTS

12 dried anchovies, guts removed

2 to 3 cups kimchi, chopped, plus brine

2 strips pork belly, chopped in bite-size pieces

Salt and/or soy sauce

Freshly ground black pepper

2 to 3 garlic cloves, crushed or finely minced

¼ onion, roughly chopped

2 tablespoons gochujang

2 teaspoons gochugaru

¼ cup enoki, shiitake, or white button mushrooms, sliced (optional)

Fish cake balls (optional)

1 block firm tofu, thickly sliced in rectangular slabs

DIRECTIONS

1. Place the dried anchovies in a pot of boiling water for about 20 minutes; when the liquid turns pale yellow, remove the anchovies and strain them from the stock.

2. Place the kimchi into the pot, add the brine, and cook on medium-high heat.

3. Season the pork belly with salt and pepper.

4. Add the pork, garlic, onions, gochujang, and gochugaru to the pot. If you like, you might add other ingredients, such as mushrooms or fish cake balls.

5. Turn up the heat until it comes to a boil, then reduce to a simmer. The pork will need about 15 minutes to cook.

6. After about 5 minutes, add the tofu (then continue to cook approximately 10 more minutes).

7. Taste your broth and season with salt or soy sauce, according to your preference.

8. Serve with a bowl of rice and enjoy!

MY FAMILY RECIPE

ABOUT MY DISH

Makes _____ servings

Prep time: _____ / Cook time: _____

INGREDIENTS

_____   _____
_____   _____
_____   _____
_____   _____
_____   _____
_____   _____
_____   _____

DIRECTIONS

THIS OR THAT?

Bite to Eat

Circle the food in each pair you are most likely to be caught reaching for.

Breakfast	←-- or --→	Dinner
Pizza	←-- or --→	Pasta
Fruit	←-- or --→	Veggies
Side of Fries	←-- or --→	Side Salad
Butter Popcorn	←-- or --→	Cheese Popcorn
Sweet	←-- or --→	Salty
Chocolate	←-- or --→	Vanilla
Cake	←-- or --→	Pie
Take-Out	←-- or --→	Home-Cooked

52

DISH OF THE DAY

You are opening a restaurant. Plan your menu below based on your favorite foods.

5 DELICIOUS
Meals

1. _____
2. _____
3. _____
4. _____
5. _____

5 SATISFYING
Snacks

1. _____
2. _____
3. _____
4. _____
5. _____

5 SWEET
Treats

1. _____
2. _____
3. _____
4. _____
5. _____

ALL WE CAN EAT

ALL over the world, families bond over what's for dinner. The foods we cook and eat together often reflect our family's culture and heritage. What does your family like to cook, bake, and eat together?

Complete the bracket to discover your favorite family food! See page 43 for how to play.

⭐ **WINNER!**

My all-time favorite family food:

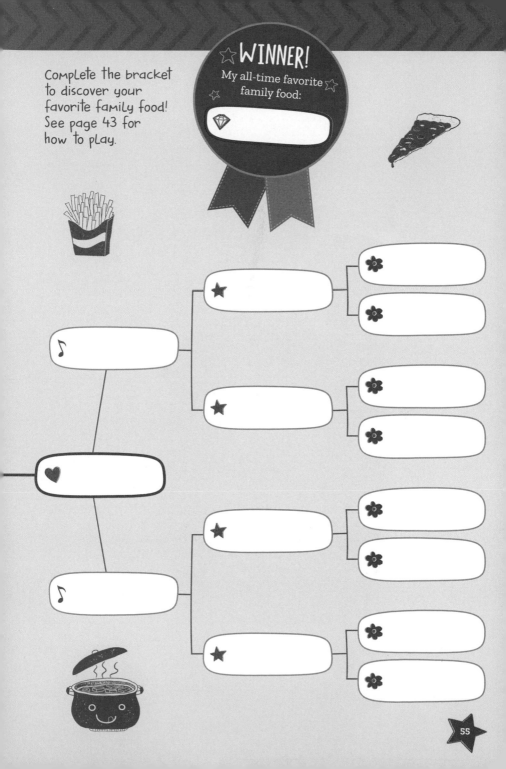

55

NOT MY TASTE

What is a food you can't stand but
everyone else seems to love?

NO PLACE LIKE HOME

What is your fave spot in your apartment or house and why?

THROUGH MY EYES

Take a look around your room and draw what you see.
Point out what makes your room uniquely you!

ALL ABOUT MY ROOM

It's been a long day. You plop down on your bed, take a deep breath, and look around. What makes your room **YOU**?

Describe Your **ROOM**

- ....
- ....
- ....
- ....
- ....

Your **FAVORITE** Things

- ....
- ....
- ....
- ....
- ....

Things You **WANT** ☆

- ....
- ....
- ....
- ....
- ....

☆

CHECK IT OFF ☑

We all have stuff we *have* to do. Finishing responsibilities feels so much better when you check them off a list. Write your responsibilities below and keep these lists handy!

DAILY

- ☐ ....
- ☐ ....
- ☐ ....
- ☐ ....
- ☐ ....

WEEKLY

- ☐ ....
- ☐ ....
- ☐ ....
- ☐ ....
- ☐ ....

MONTHLY

- ☐ ....
- ☐ ....
- ☐ ....
- ☐ ....
- ☐ ....

MOST VALUABLE PET

Share the greatest pet story
you can think of.

Draw or paste
a picture here!

WHAT IS YOUR PERFECT PET?

Are you a cat person or a dog person? Or something else entirely? Take the quiz to find out what pet matches your personality!

 Your family says you are
   a. chill.   **b.** independent.   **c.** lovable.

 Surprise! You got the perfect present. It is
   a. cool stuff for your room.
   b. a great book to read.
   c. a game to play with your friends.

 You have the most energy in the
   a. afternoon.   **b.** evening.   **c.** morning.

 On sunny days, you are
   a. hanging out in your room.
   b. exploring the neighborhood.
   c. at the park.

Pick one!

 a.   b.   c.

 At sleepovers, you choose to
   a. sleep! What else?
   b. play harmless pranks.
   c. get the popcorn and watch a movie.

 Your dancing style is
   a. swaying back and forth.
   b. fast, fun moves.
   c. always better with a group!

 On social media, you most enjoy the
   a. pretty photos.   b. latest memes.   c. funny videos.

 At bedtime, your favorite moment is
   a. falling asleep.
   b. curling up under a blanket.
   c. hugging your family good night.

Count how many A's, B's, and C's you chose
on the quiz to reveal your perfect pet!

A	B	C

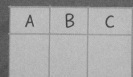

RESULTS! YOUR PET IS A . . .

MOSTLY A'S ☐

Put a check next to your perfect pet!

FISH

Prepare for the **CHILLEST** pet ever! **CALM** and **COOL**, a fish will enjoy the little things and is always **READY TO LISTEN** to your deepest thoughts.

MOSTLY B'S ☐

CAT

Cats are **SMART** and **INDEPENDENT**—just like you! Life with a cat is full of **LOVE** and lots of **SURPRISES**. You will have **FUN** seeing what your cat is up to next.

MOSTLY C'S ☐

DOG

You are in for a lot of **CUDDLING** and possibly **SLOBBERING**, too. A dog is a **GREAT** and **LOYAL** friend and **ADVENTURER**, especially when there's food involved!

QUIZ REFLECTION

Color in the bar to show how much you agree with your quiz results on a scale of 1-10.

| 1 | 2 | 3 | 4 | 5 | 6 | 7 | 8 | 9 | 10 |

Absolutely not!   Makes sense.   Exactly right!

What did the quiz get RIGHT?

What did the quiz get WRONG?

SHARE THE QUIZ!

Which pet should your family and friends get? Ask them to take the quiz, and then fill in their results below.

NAME	PERFECT PET IS . . .

Name: Helen Charlotte Pelroy

Nickname: Sailboat Girl

Age: 12

Birthday: September 27th

Favorite Color: gold and lavender

Favorite Food: pasta and chocolate chip cookies

Favorite Animal: panda

Hobbies: basketball, crafts, and hanging with friends

3 Adjectives to Describe Them: curious, kind, and charming

ABOUT
MY BEST
FRIEND

Attach or draw
a picture of your
best friend here!

Name: ....

Nickname: ....

Age: ....

Birthday: ....

Favorite Color: ....

Favorite Food: ....

Favorite Animal: ....

Hobbies: ....

3 Adjectives to Describe Them: ....

ABOUT PIPPA'S OLDEST FRIEND

Name: Buddy Benjamin Johnson

Nickname:

Age: 12

Birthday: May 8th

Favorite Color: green

Favorite Food: pretzels and potato chips

Favorite Animal: armadillo

Hobbies: basketball, video games, and movies

3 Adjectives to Describe Them: easygoing, enthusiastic, and friendly

ABOUT MY OLDEST FRIEND

Attach or draw a picture of your oldest friend here!

Name: _____

Nickname: _____

Age: _____

Birthday: _____

Favorite Color: _____

Favorite Food: _____

Favorite Animal: _____

Hobbies: _____

3 Adjectives to Describe Them: _____

_____

ABOUT PIPPA'S ROLE MODEL*

*A friend you really look up to!

Name: Matthew Lucas Haverford

Nickname:

Age: 17

Birthday: March 2nd

Favorite Color: green

Favorite Food: cakes and candy

Favorite Animal: swan

Hobbies: listening to and playing music

3 Adjectives to Describe Them: artistic, daring, and gentle

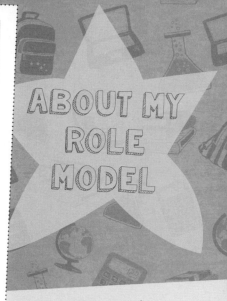

ABOUT MY ROLE MODEL

Attach or draw a picture of your role model here!

Name: ....

Nickname: ....

Age: ....

Birthday: ....

Favorite Color: ....

Favorite Food: ....

Favorite Animal: ....

Hobbies: ....

3 Adjectives to Describe Them: ....

....

NEVER A DULL MOMENT

Life is better and brighter because of best friends and the time you spend together. How do you spend time with your friends?

THINGS We Do

- _____
- _____
- _____
- _____
- _____

PLACES We Go

- _____
- _____
- _____
- _____
- _____

STUFF We Talk About

- _____
- _____
- _____
- _____
- _____

THE BEST OF FRIENDS

Brag about your best friends and everything that makes them so great.

Draw or paste a picture here!

MEMORIES FOR DAYS

LOL!

Inside jokes, shoulders to cry on, and everything in between—friends are the best. Fill in the hearts with your favorite friendship memories.

THROUGH THICK AND THIN

Think of a time you felt the most loved
by your friends. What happened?

_____

_____

_____

_____

_____

_____

_____

_____

_____

_____

_____

_____

_____

BRING OUT
THE BESTIE IN ME

Share a time when you were a good friend.

WHICH *PIPPA PARK* CHARACTER WOULD BE YOUR BFF?

Pippa Park is surrounded by friends who challenge, support, and celebrate her. Take the quiz to find out which *Pippa Park Raises Her Game* character would be your BFF.

 When something wonderful happens to you, you
  a. can't stop talking about it, even if you try.
  b. are all smiles, and it's contagious!
  c. look for fun ways to celebrate.

 Your friends would describe you as
  a. talkative.   b. kind.   c. ambitious.

 But your friends would never call you
  a. a closed book.   b. rowdy.   c. negative.

 The score is tied during the last basketball game of the season with three seconds left on the clock. You have the ball and
  a. take the three-point shot even if you might miss.
  b. pass it to the best open player and switch to defense.
  c. call a time-out to strategize with the team.

5 Your superhero power would be
   a. shape-shifting.   **b.** mind reading.   **c.** flying.

 6 It's Friday! School's out! You and your friends are
   a. trying the newest face masks and self-care trends.
   b. baking, crafting, or making something new.
   c. planning your next adventure.

 7 What do you believe to be most true?
   a. What goes around comes around.
   b. Two wrongs don't make a right.
   c. Don't judge a book by its cover.

 8 When you see your crush, you
   a. ask your friends for advice.
   b. shyly wave hello.
   c. run up and start a conversation.

 9 Your texts are most likely to include
   a. emojis.
   b. LOLs.
   c. exclamation points!

Count how many A's, B's, and C's you chose on the quiz to reveal which *Pippa Park* character would be your best friend.

A	B	C

RESULTS! YOUR BFF IS . . .

MOSTLY A'S ☐

← Put a check next your *Pippa Park BFF!*

CAROLINE

She is a **LOYAL** and **PROUD** sidekick who will tell you the truth **NO MATTER WHAT**. It may be hard to hear sometimes, but she wants the best for you and is **ALWAYS** on your side!

MOSTLY B'S ☐

HELEN

She is **WARM** and **WELCOMING** right from the start! Her **KINDNESS** and **CHARM** will help you through the hardest times and make the good ones **EVEN SWEETER**.

MOSTLY C'S ☐

MATTHEW

He is **DARING** yet **WISE**, the perfect friend to **SUPPORT** you in your own **ADVENTURES**. Go after your dreams with **CONFIDENCE**, knowing you have someone to catch you if you fall.

QUIZ REFLECTION

Color in the bar to show how much you agree with your
quiz results on a scale of 1-10.

| 1 | 2 | 3 | 4 | 5 | 6 | 7 | 8 | 9 | 10 |

Absolutely not!   Makes sense.   Exactly right!

What did the quiz get **RIGHT**?   What did the quiz get **WRONG**?

-------------------------------------   -------------------------------------

-------------------------------------   -------------------------------------

-------------------------------------   -------------------------------------

SHARE THE QUIZ!

Which BFF would your family and friends get? Ask them to take
the quiz, and then fill in their results below.

NAME	BFF IS . . .

FICTIONAL FACE-OFF

Have you ever met a character in a book, TV show, or movie that you couldn't get enough of? Maybe they were just like you or perfect best-friend material.

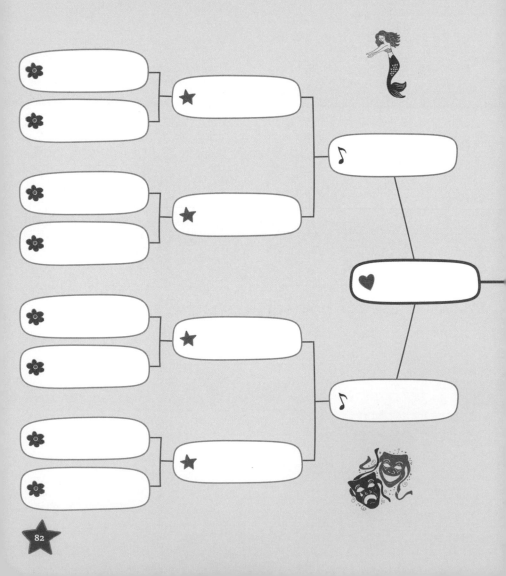

Complete the bracket to discover your favorite fictional character! See page 43 for how to play.

See page 43 for how to play.

⭐ WINNER!
My all-time favorite fictional character:

Name: Eliot Reginald Haverford

Nickname:

Age: 13

Birthday: June 13th

Hobbies: learning, puzzles, and alone time

3 Adjectives to Describe Them: smart, independent, and loyal

What do you like about them: Eliot is one of the smartest boys in the eighth grade. And although he doesn't smile often, when he does, it's pure sunlight.

ABOUT MY CRUSH

Attach or draw a picture of your crush here!

Name: _____

Nickname: _____

Age: _____

Birthday: _____

Hobbies: _____

3 Adjectives to Describe Them: _____
_____

What do you like about them: _____
_____
_____

ABOUT OTHER PIPPA'S CRUSH

Name: Marvel Lucas Moon

Nickname:

Age: 12

Birthday: February 21st

Hobbies: video games, tennis, and listening to music

3 Adjectives to Describe Them: energetic, funny, and bold

What do you like about them: Marvel is hilarious and always makes me laugh. Plus, he has excellent taste in K-pop.

ABOUT OTHER MY CRUSH

Attach or draw a picture of your <u>other</u> crush here!

Name: ....

Nickname: ....

Age: ....

Birthday: ....

Hobbies: ....

3 Adjectives to Describe Them: ....

....

What do you like about them: ....

....

....

CRUSHIN' IT

Maybe you *Like* Like someone or maybe you don't. If you have ever Liked someone as more than a friend, what qualities made you think of that person in that way?

What Catches **YOUR EYE**?

- ♥ ....
- ♥ ....
- ♥ ....
- ♥ ....
- ♥ ....

What Makes You Look the **OTHER WAY**?

- ♥ ....
- ♥ ....
- ♥ ....
- ♥ ....
- ♥ ....

Celebrity **CRUSHES**

1. ....
2. ....
3. ....
4. ....
5. ....

CATCH YOUR EYE

When you meet someone new, what is the first thing you notice?

MAKING SCHOOL COOL

What is the HIGHLIGHT of your school day?

TEACHER'S PET

Who is your favorite teacher **EVER** and why?

Your secret is safe with me!

THIS OR THAT?

Change of Subject

Circle your favorite school subject in each of the following pairs.

Math	⟵ or ⟶	Language Arts
Reading	⟵ or ⟶	Writing
Art	⟵ or ⟶	Phys Ed
Science	⟵ or ⟶	History
Drama	⟵ or ⟶	Choir
French	⟵ or ⟶	Spanish
Yearbook	⟵ or ⟶	School Paper
Computer Lab	⟵ or ⟶	Band

 BONUS QUESTION Bring Lunch ⟵ or ⟶ Buy Lunch

STUDENT LIFE

School is much more than just a place for learning. It's a place for making memories.

Things in My
BACKPACK

- _____
- _____
- _____
- _____
- _____

TEACHERS
I'll Never Forget

- _____
- _____
- _____
- _____
- _____

CLUBS I'm In
(Or Can't Wait to Join!)

- _____
- _____
- _____
- _____
- _____

PAGE TURNER

Embrace your inner bookworm. Fill in the lists below to keep track of books that left a lasting impression on you.

No rush! Add books as you read them.

 Books That **MAKE ME LAUGH**

1. ....
2. ....
3. ....
4. ....
5. ....

Books That **MAKE ME CRY**

1. ....
2. ....
3. ....
4. ....
5. ....

Books That Are **SPECIAL TO ME**

1. ....
2. ....
3. ....
4. ....
5. ....

YOU'RE THE AUTHOR!

If you wrote a book, what would it be about?

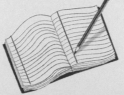

BEST BOOK EVER

Think about the books that popped off the pages, turned words into worlds, and introduced you to new experiences. Which books were Like that for you?

Complete the bracket to discover the best book ever! See page 43 for how to play.

WINNER!
The best book ever:

IT HAPPENS TO THE BEST OF US

Think about a time when you felt embarrassed. What happened?

LAUGH IT OFF

One of the best ways to get over embarrassment is to laugh about it. So . . . what was funny about the situation?

ALL THE FEELS!

Everyone has bad feelings sometimes. What pick-me-ups do you use when you're feeling down? Fill in the bubbles with things that bring a smile back to your face.

ONE BRAVE DAY

Think of a time you courageously faced a challenge. What happened? Draw that day as a superhero comic below. After all, you are the hero of your own story.

TITLE:

DON'T FORGET TO INCLUDE YOUR REAL-LIFE SIDEKICKS!

WHAT AFTER-SCHOOL ACTIVITY SHOULD YOU TRY?

School's out for the day! Take the quiz to find out what activity you should check out next!

 1 Your favorite things to talk about are
   a. movies, shows, and books.
   b. what is going on in the world.
   c. the latest and greatest sports news.

 2 Your after-school activity should challenge you to be more
   a. imaginative.   **b.** prepared.   **c.** competitive.

 3 Your homework plan of attack is to
   a. work on multiple assignments at the same time.
   b. finish it in class.
   c. call your friends over to work on it together.

 4 Your favorite class is
   a. Language Arts.   **b.** History.   **c.** Phys Ed.

5. The best part of watching sports is
  a. the halftime show.
  b. predicting the winning team.
  c. all of it! What's not to love?

 6. It's your turn to choose a game for game night! You go with
  a. charades.   **b.** trivia.   **c.** dodgeball.

 7. If you were an animal, you would be a
  a. proud peacock.   **b.** clever fox.   **c.** brave lion.

 8. You sign up for the school play. Your role is
  a. the lead, of course!
  b. head writer and script coordinator.
  c. a stagehand working behind the scenes.

 9. When you grow up, you want to be a(n)
  a. actor.   **b.** lawyer.   **b.** athlete.

Count how many A's, B's, and C's you chose on the quiz to reveal what after-school activity you should try next!

A	B	C

MOSTLY A'S ☐

Put a check next to your next after-school activity!

THEATER GROUP

Your **CREATIVITY** and **CONFIDENCE** make you perfect for the theater. Some people say **DRAMATIC** like it's a bad thing, but you appreciate a good story—even better when you're the **STAR**!

MOSTLY B'S ☐

DEBATE CLUB

Your **QUICK WIT** and **CURIOSITY** make debate the **LOGICAL** next step! Plus, you love hanging with your **FRIENDS** and **LEARNING** new things, and debate is the **BEST** of both worlds.

MOSTLY C'S ☐

SPORTS TEAM

Your **OUTGOING** and **COMPETITIVE** nature makes you an ideal athlete. Regardless of your athletic ability, your **POSITIVE ENERGY** and **CAN-DO ATTITUDE** make any team **LUCKY** to have you.

Color in the bar to show how much you agree with your quiz results on a scale of 1-10.

1	2	3	4	5	6	7	8	9	10

Absolutely not!   Makes sense.   Exactly right!

What did the quiz get **RIGHT**?   What did the quiz get **WRONG**?

-------------------------------------   -------------------------------------

-------------------------------------   -------------------------------------

-------------------------------------   -------------------------------------

SHARE THE QUIZ!

Which new activity should your family and friends try? Ask them to take the quiz, and then fill in their results below.

NAME	NEW ACTIVITY IS . . .

THE SCHOOL BELL RINGS . . .

What now? What is your after-school routine?

_____

_____

_____

_____

_____

_____

_____

_____

_____

_____

_____

_____

SIGN UP!

Are you involved in any activities
outside of school? Which ones?

← Draw or paste
a picture here!

MY HOMETOWN

What are your favorite places in town? What do you love about them? Fill in the buildings with words or drawings of all the places that make your town feel like **HOME**.

ABOUT PIPPA'S SQUAD

MEET BIANCA

Name: Bianca Ava Davis #33

Birthday: August 18th

3 Adjectives to Describe Them:
confident, driven, and intelligent

They are a good teammate because . . .
she's a strong leader who isn't afraid
to make tough calls.

MEET OLIVE

Name: Olive Stella Giordano #8

Birthday: November 19th

3 Adjectives to Describe Them:
talkative, eager, and sneaky

They are a good teammate because . . .
she practices hard and is always
improving her skills.

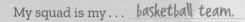

My squad is my... basketball team.

MEET CAROLINE

Name: Caroline Isabella Bingham #23

Birthday: October 28th

3 Adjectives to Describe Them:
fashionable, proud, and honest

They are a good teammate because...
she is the fastest player on the court.

MEET WINONA

Name: Winona "Win" Hussein #14

Birthday: January 6th

3 Adjectives to Describe Them:
responsible, shy, and relaxed

They are a good teammate because...
she has fast instincts and can adapt
to any situation.

ABOUT MY SQUAD

Name: _____

Birthday: _____

3 Adjectives to Describe Them: _____

_____

They are a good teammate because . . .

_____

_____

_____

Name: _____

Birthday: _____

3 Adjectives to Describe Them: _____

_____

They are a good teammate because . . .

_____

_____

_____

My squad is my . . .

Name:

Birthday:

3 Adjectives to Describe Them:

They are a good teammate because . . .

Attach or draw pictures of your squad!

Name:

Birthday:

3 Adjectives to Describe Them:

They are a good teammate because . . .

Time to Shine!

Have you ever felt like the star of the show, the field, or even just your living room? Shine a spotlight on that moment by drawing it in the spaces below.

TITLE: _____

TRY IMAGINING IT ONSTAGE, AND TRANSFORM IT FOR THE THEATER!

WOULD YOU RATHER?

School's Out

You just finished a long day of school. Circle the item in each pair that best reflects how you spend your time.

Plan Everything Go with the Flow

Your House Friend's House

Homework Right After School Homework? Later . . .

Text Your Friends Back Right Away Take your Time Responding

Captain of Sports Team Lead in School Play

Sing in the Choir Dance with a Squad

Outside Adventures Stay Indoors

Arts & Crafts Games & Tech

★ STAR QUALITY ★

If you could grow up to become famous, what would you want to be famous for?

WHICH TEAM AWARD SHOULD YOU WIN?

A great team needs all kinds of different players, and the MVP shouldn't get all the credit. Take the quiz to find out which team award has your name on it!

 1 Your go-to movie genre is
   a. comedy.   **b.** drama.   **c.** superhero.

 2 When your best friend is having a bad day, you
   a. try to make them smile.
   b. listen to their thoughts and feelings.
   c. share encouraging pieces of advice.

 3 For group projects, you
   a. lead the presentation.
   b. pick up the slack when needed.
   c. plan who is doing what.

 4 Pick one!

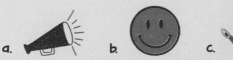
  a.   **b.**   **c.**

5 Your teachers say you are
    a. entertaining.   **b.** helpful.   **c.** independent.

 6 At the school dance, you are
    a. starting a dance-off.
    b. joining a dance circle with friends.
    c. requesting all the best songs.

 7 Your top emoji is the
    a. heart eyes.   **b.** blushing smile.   **c.** thumbs-up.

 8 Road trip! You're in charge of the
    a. entertainment! Music, games, and fun conversation.
    b. car snacks! Don't forget the drinks, too.
    c. fun pit stops! You know exactly where Mom will want to stop.

9 Your feelings are
    a. on your sleeve for the world to see.
    b. shared with only your closest friends.
    c. channeled into the game.

Count how many A, B, and C's you chose on the quiz to reveal your team award on the next page!

A	B	C

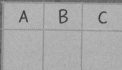

CONGRATS! YOU WON . . .

MOSTLY A'S ☐

← Put a check next to your team award!

SPIRIT LEADER

Your **TEAM PRIDE** and **ENTHUSIASM** are off the charts! You know how to keep your team's **SPIRITS UP** whether you win or lose, and your **POSITIVITY** is contagious.

MOSTLY B'S ☐

HUMBLE BEE

You don't need to be a star to be a **STAR**. You are **KIND** and **HELPFUL**, no questions asked. Your friends know you as the **GLUE** that holds **EVERYTHING** together.

MOSTLY C'S ☐

TEAM CAPTAIN

You are a **NATURAL-BORN LEADER**, and your teammates know they can count on you! You have a true **LOVE** for the game, and because of your **CONFIDENCE**, no one can **EVER** doubt you.

QUIZ REFLECTION

Color in the bar to show how much you agree with your
quiz results on a scale of 1-10.

| 1 | 2 | 3 | 4 | 5 | 6 | 7 | 8 | 9 | 10 |

Absolutely not!   Makes sense.   Exactly right!

What did the quiz get **RIGHT**?

What did the quiz get **WRONG**?

SHARE THE QUIZ!

Which team award would your family and friends get? Ask them
to take the quiz, and then fill in their results below.

NAME	TEAM AWARD IS . . .

ALL FUN AND GAMES

☑ School
☑ Homework
☑ Chores

Responsibilities are taken care of. What now? How do you most like to spend your free time?

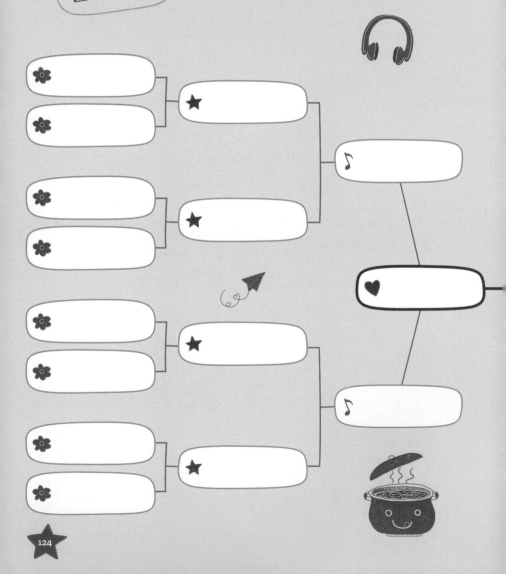

Complete the bracket to discover your favorite thing to do! See page 43 for how to play.

ULTIMATE PLAYLIST

Let's create a soundtrack for your Life. What songs are on it? FiLL in the Lists beLow with Music that's Made for you!

Songs I Know **EVERY WORD** To

♪ ....
♪ ....
♪ ....
♪ ....
♪ ....

Songs I **GET STUCK** in My Head

♪ ....
♪ ....
♪ ....
♪ ....
♪ ....

Songs I Secretly Like . . . **SHHH!**

♪ ....
♪ ....
♪ ....
♪ ....
♪ ....

MY ANTHEM

Think of what lyrics stand out to you!

If you could pick the perfect theme song for your life, what would it be?

TV TIME

You have a big bowl of popcorn, a cozy blanket, and the remote. You press play. What comes up on the TV?

Favorite
TV SHOWS

- ....
- ....
- ....
- ....
- ....

Favorite
MOVIES

- ....
- ....
- ....
- ....
- ....

Favorite
VIDEO GAMES

- ....
- ....
- ....
- ....
- ....

JUST LIKE ME

How is your Life Like
your favorite TV show?

↑ Draw or paste
a picture here!

THE GREAT INDOORS

You are creating the ideal video game.
Draw the cover below!

Video games not your thing? Draw a movie, album, or book cover instead!

THE GREAT OUTDOORS

Where do you feel most connected to nature?

Think about what you see and hear when you are there!

WOULD YOU RATHER?

When I Grow Up . . .

Circle the career in each pair that sounds more interesting to you.

Actor	‹‒‒‒ or ‒‒‒›	Doctor
Business Owner	‹‒‒‒ or ‒‒‒›	Pro Athlete
Chef	‹‒‒‒ or ‒‒‒›	Astronaut
Author	‹‒‒‒ or ‒‒‒›	Police Officer
Pilot	‹‒‒‒ or ‒‒‒›	Vet
Teacher	‹‒‒‒ or ‒‒‒›	Dancer
Musician	‹‒‒‒ or ‒‒‒›	Scientist
Nurse	‹‒‒‒ or ‒‒‒›	Fashion Designer
Librarian	‹‒‒‒ or ‒‒‒›	Firefighter

#GOALS

What do you want to be when you grow up and why?

CHANGE THE WORLD

How would you change the world if you could?

FUTURE YOU!

Close your eyes and imagine you jumped ahead to the future. What does your future hold? Open your eyes and fill in all the possibilities.

DREAM PLACES
to Live

1. _____
2. _____
3. _____
4. _____
5. _____

DREAM JOBS

1. _____
2. _____
3. _____
4. _____
5. _____

GOALS
for Future You

1. _____
2. _____
3. _____
4. _____
5. _____

DREAM **BIG!**

MY LiFe CHeCKLiSt

You can do anything you put your mind to! Write or draw a checklist of goals you hope to achieve in the future.

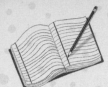

LETTER TO MY FUTURE SELF

Think about your hopes and dreams for the future. Capture those thoughts in a letter to your future self.

Date _____

Dear _____

PIPPA PARK RAISES HER GAME
BOOK CLUB

The only thing more satisfying than reading a really great book is getting to gush over it with your friends. Use these questions to start your very own book club with *Pippa Park Raises Her Game* by Erin Yun.

BOOK CLUB MEMBERS:

Pippa Park Raises Her Game Rating:

I gave this rating because . . . _____

_____

_____

_____

DISCUSSION QUESTIONS

1. Pippa isn't an orphan, but at times she feels like one. Describe Pippa's relationship with Mina, her older sister. Why is Mina so tough on Pippa? Discuss whether Mina resents taking care of Pippa. How is Jung-Hwa, Mina's husband, a father figure to Pippa? How does he make Pippa feel better after she has a fight with Mina?

2. What is the definition of family? Explain why Pippa's mother had to return to Korea. How are Mina and Jung-Hwa realizing the American dream? Discuss how Pippa's family situation is similar to that of new Americans throughout the nation. How are many of them separated from their loved ones? Discuss why it's important to celebrate all types of families.

3. Pippa says, "At Lakeview I could be anyone, as long as they didn't find out the truth about me." What doesn't she want the kids at Lakeview to know about her? What does she do to keep her home life private? What does Pippa think would happen if the girls found out the truth about her?

4. How does trying to fit in cause Pippa to lose her sense of self? Why is she ashamed of her family and the way they live? At the end of the novel, Pippa invites the basketball team to her apartment. What is significant about this gesture?

Pippa's best friend at Victoria Middle is Buddy Johnson. Think about how she betrays him. Discuss an apology and explanation for her behavior that she might give to Buddy.

 Why does Pippa think that Eliot's family life is more messed up than hers? How does knowing about his family make her better understand Eliot? At what point does Mr. Haverford gain the courage to stand up to Aunt Evelyn?

 Olive Giordano is the student ambassador that shows Pippa around the school. How does Olive's desire to be popular affect her judgment and turn her into a cyberbully? When Pippa learns that Olive is Throwaway, how does that make Pippa feel? Discuss cyberbullying in your school.

 Discuss what Jung-Hwa means when he says, "The lower you fall, the more room you have to rise." What is Pippa's lowest point? How do you know that she is about to rise? Have you ever felt the same way?

9 Pippa's family celebrates Chuseok: Korean Thanksgiving Day. Learn more about the traditions associated with this holiday on the Internet. Describe and discuss the holiday and the food that is prepared. What cultural holidays does your family celebrate? Is there anything special that you eat?

 10 *Pippa Park Raises Her Game* is a contemporary reimagining of *Great Expectations*. Use books or the Internet to find out about the main characters in *Great Expectations*. What is each character's counterpart in *Pippa Park Raises Her Game*? List the characters side by side, and as a group, apply two or three adjectives that best describe each of them.

 11 Think about all that has happened to Pippa. Then consider the following quote from *Great Expectations*: "And it was not until I began to think, that I began fully to know how wrecked I was, and how the ship in which I had sailed was gone to pieces." What is the metaphorical ship that Pippa sails? At what point does Pippa realize "how wrecked" her life is? How does she turn her life around once she begins "thinking"?

 12 If you were to pick one character from *Pippa Park Raises Her Game* who is most like you, who would it be and why? Who is most unlike you and why? Which character from the book would you want as your friend and why?

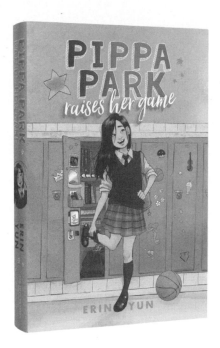